the weather

pour Robert

the weather _(lucretian)_

LISA ROBERTSON

Lisa R.

vancouver
new star books
2007

NEW STAR BOOKS LTD.
107 - 3477 Commercial Street   Vancouver, BC   V5N 4E8   CANADA
1574 Gulf Road, #1517   Point Roberts, WA 98281   USA
www.NewStarBooks.com   info@NewStarBooks.com

Publication of this work is made possible by the support of the Canada
Council, the Department of Canadian Heritage Book Publishing Industry
Development Program, the British Columbia Arts Council, and the British
Columbia Book Publishing Tax Credit.

Cover: Robin Mitchell / Steedman Design
First published 2001. Reprinted 2003, 2007
Printed and bound in Canada by Gauvin Press

CANADIAN CATALOGUING IN PUBLICATION DATA

Robertson, Lisa
  The weather

  Poems.
  ISBN 0-921586-81-7

  I. Title.
PS8585.03217W42 2001   C811´.54   C2001-910376-X
PS9199.3.R5316W42 2001

Architecture, fashion – yes, even the weather – are, in the interior of the collective, what the sensoria of organs, the feeling of sickness or health, are in the individual. . . . They stand in the cycle of the eternally selfsame, until the collective seizes upon them in politics and history emerges.

WALTER BENJAMIN, **THE ARCADES PROJECT**

sunday

About here. All along here. All along here. All the soft coercions. Maybe black and shiny, wrinkled. A sky marbled with failures. A patterned revision. And got here about one o'clock. And got here wet to the skin. And here are houses too, here and there. And luck, too, whenever. And here experienced the benefits. And here again wisps. And here gained real knowledge. And here got into the wild. And here, too. Arrived here about two o'clock. Here alone the length. There is a bed of chalk under this. The fresh water falls here. Clumps of lofty trees. Dictions of deficit. Maybe we bristle. Came at the fact here. Everything has been done here. Every system's torn or roughened. Every surface discontinuous. Everywhere we are tipping our throats back, streaming and sifting. Got at work here, streaming and sifting. Got here to breakfast. Got here to sleep. Here a streak of light, there a streak of dark. Here and there a house. Here are all of the causes.

Maybe a flesh that reverses. Here are farms and manors and mines and woods and forests and houses and streets. Here are hill and dell. Here are hill, dell, water, meadows, woods. Line upon line the twist and luck. Here are new enclosures. The chalk and the sand. Here are two. Here tongues. Here be nameless. Here has been the squandering. Here has been the work. Here we close the day. Here upon the edge. Here is a basin. A canal. A church. Here is a church. Here is a deep loam upon chalk. Here is a hill. Here is a house. Here is a system. Time pours from its mouth. We design it a flickering. Here is its desolation. Here it crosses. Here it falls at last. Here it has its full gratification. Here on the yet visible remains. The first. Maybe this gaze. Here, waiting. Here it crossed. Here, close along. Quit some causes. Here, then. Here were a set. Here were two or three. So deliciously alterior. Here will be an interchange of cause and effect. Here, as everywhere else. In this tranquil spot. Here, Pete. Delicate perspex articulations. Twisting and passing. High along here. Ate here. Came here. Got here after deviations. Got here at nine o'clock. Coming here to remain here. Maybe we were frightened. And then go back. We speak from memory here all the way along. Whenever. On a pivot. Without conclusivity. Stopped here and there. Endeavoured. Here mentioned. In short, not here. Maybe we disproved theories. It is a beautiful bed of earth. It is along here. It is impossible not to recollect. It was here. Towards the west. Towards a zone of dormancy. Towards the very beautiful frieze of the lyric class. Towards the frieze of undone agency. Towards the modern. Maybe in shade. No great things along here. No hard treatment of them here. People ought to be happy. So good as it is here. So that here is a falling off. Some of us love its common and at times accidental beauty. Springs start here and there. Streams sift chop up spit out knots or clouds. Still there are some spots here and there. Stuck up here. Such are all the places along here. The thing is not done here. The thing will not stop. There as well as here streams sifts chops up spits out twists passes and too remains. The hour has reached its peak. There being here a sort of dell. There has been rain here. Maybe pointed and folding. There is law here all languid and lax. These are the subject of conversation. They have begun to trust here. Passing and remaining and awaiting. This has been a sad time all along here yet full of a detailed lust. Trees are nearly as big here. Two branches meet. Very little along here. Here upon a bed of chalk. Got here about three o'clock. There was an alterior atmosphere. What a pretty thing it is.

It was Jessica Grim the American poet
who first advised me to read Violette Leduc.
Lurid conditions are facts. This is no different
from the daily protests and cashbars.
I now unknowingly speed towards
which of all acts, words, conditions —
I am troubled that I do not know.
When I feel depressed in broad daylight
depressed by the disappearance of names, the pollen
smearing the windowsill, I picture
the bending pages of *La Bâtarde*
and I think of wind. The outspread world is

comparable to a large theatre
or to rending paper, and the noise it makes when it flaps
is riotous. Clothes swish through the air, rubbing
my ears. Promptly I am quenched. I'm talking
about a cheap paperback which fans and
slips to the floor with a shush. Skirt stretched
taut between new knees, head turned back, I
hold down a branch,

monday

First all belief is paradise. So pliable a medium. A time not very long. A transparency caused. A conveyance of rupture. A subtle transport. Scant and rare. Deep in the opulent morning, blissful regions, hard and slender. Scarce and scant. Quotidian and temperate. Begin afresh in the realms of the atmosphere, that encompasses the solid earth, the terraqueous globe that soars and sings, elevated and flimsy. Bright and hot. Flesh and hue. Our skies are inventions, durations, discoveries, quotas, forgeries, fine and grand. Fine and grand. Fresh and bright. Heavenly and bright. The day pours out space, a light red roominess, bright and fresh. Bright and oft. Bright and fresh. Sparkling and wet. Clamour and tint. We range the spacious fields, a battlement trick and fast. Bright and silver. Ribbons and failings. To and fro. Fine and grand. The sky is complicated and flawed and we're up there in it, floating near the apricot frill, the bias swoop, near the

sullen bloated part that dissolves to silver the next instant
bronze but nothing that meaningful, a breach of greeny-
blue, a syllable, we're all across the swathe of fleece laid
out, the fraying rope, the copper beech behind the
aluminum catalpa that has saved the entire spring for this
flight, the tops of these a part of the sky, the light wind
flipping up the white undersides of leaves, heaven afresh,
the brushed part behind, the tumbling. So to the heavenly
rustling. Just stiff with ambition we range the spacious
trees in earnest desire sure and dear. Brisk and west.
Streaky and massed. Changing and appearing. First and
last. This was made from Europe, formed from Europe,
rant and roar. Fine and grand. Fresh and bright. Crested
and turbid. Silver and bright. This was spoken as it came
to us, to celebrate and tint, distinct and designed. Sure and
dear. Fully designed. Dear afresh. So free to the showing.
What we praise we believe, we fully believe. Very fine.

Belief thin and pure and clear to the title. Very beautiful. Belief lovely and elegant and fair for the footing. Very brisk. Belief lively and quick and strong by the bursting. Very bright. Belief clear and witty and famous in impulse. Very stormy. Belief violent and open and raging from privation. Very fine. Belief intransigent after pursuit. Very hot. Belief lustful and eager and curious before beauty. Very bright. Belief intending afresh. So calmly and clearly. Just stiff with leaf sure and dear and appearing and last. With lust clear and scarce and appearing and last and afresh.

Give me hackneyed words because
they are good. Brocade me the whole body
of terrestrial air. Say spongy ground
with its soft weeds. Say self because it can.
Say arts of happiness. Say you have died.
Say sequin because the word just
appeared. Say weather take this adult
from its box. Memorize being sequined
to something, water. Everything you forget
inserts love into the silent money.
Memorize huge things of girders greased. Say
the water parting about the particular
animal. Say what happens to the face
as it gala tints my simple cut
vicious this afternoon the beautiful
light on the cash is human to guzzle
with — go away wild feelings, there you go
as the robin as the songsparrow go
the system shines with uninterrupted

light. It's petal caked. Leaves shoot up. Each
leaf's a runnel. Far into the night a
sweetness. Marvelous. Spectacular. Brilliant.
Clouded towards the south. It translates
Lucretius. Say cup of your heart rush
sluice is yellow sluice Kate Moss is Rousseau
have my arms. Say impasto of
atmosphere for her fur. Halo open
her face. Misplace the death. All the truth
under the tree has two pinky oozy
names. Say trying to possess or not. Say
if you thought love was ironical. If
pleasure emancipates, why aren't you some-
where. Sincerity.

tuesday

Days heap upon us. All plain. All clouds except a narrow opening at the top of the sky. All cloudy except a narrow opening at the bottom of the sky with others smaller. All cloudy except a narrow opening at the bottom of the sky. All cloudy except a narrow opening at the top of the sky. All cloudy. All cloudy. All cloudy. Except one large opening with others smaller. And once in the clouds. Days heap upon us. Where is our anger. And the shades darker than the plain part and darker at the top than the bottom. But darker at bottom than top. Days heap upon us. Where is Ti-Grace. But darker at the bottom than the top. Days heap upon us. Where is Christine. Broken on the word culture. But darker at the bottom than the top. Days heap upon us. Where is Valerie. Pulling the hard air into her lung. The life crumbles open. But darker at the bottom than the top. Days heap upon us. Where is Patty. Unlearning each thing. Red sky crumbles open. This is the only way to expand the heart. But darker at the top than the bottom. Days heap upon us. Where is Shulamith. Abolishing the word love. The radical wing crumbles open. The scorn is not anticipated. We have given our surface. Darker at the top than the bottom. Except one large opening with others smaller. Except one large opening with others smaller. Gradually. Days heap upon us. Where is Patricia. In the dream of obedience and authority. The genitalia crumble open. It is only ever a flickering. We never worshipped grief. It has been stuccoed over. Half cloud half plain. Half cloud half plain. Half plain. One in the plain part and one in the clouds. Days heap upon us. Where is Jane. Looking for food. Hunger crumbles open. All this is built on her loveliness. We have fallen into a category. Love subsidized our descent. Streaky clouds at the bottom of the sky. Days heap upon us. Where is Mary. In the extreme brevity of the history of parity. Rage crumbles open. It felt like dense fog. What is fact is not necessarily human. Memory anticipitates. Authority flows into us like a gel. We cross the border to confront the ideal. Streaky cloudy at the top of the sky. Days heap upon us. Where is Grace. Spent in sadness. The underground crumbles open. There is no transgression possible. We publicly mobilize the horror of our emotion. It is a phalanx. The clouds darker than the plain or blue part and darker at the top than the bottom. Days heap upon us. Where is Gloria. Pushing down laughter. Utopia crumbles open. It is an emotion similar to animals sporting. We won't plagiarize shame. Like this we solve herself. The clouds darker than the plain part and darker at the top than the bottom. The clouds darker than the plain part and darker at the top than the bottom. The clouds lighter than the plain part and darker at the top than the bottom. The clouds lighter than the plain part and darker at the bottom than top. The clouds lighter than the plain part and darker at the top than the bottom. The lights of the clouds lighter and the darks darker than the plain part and darker at the top than the bottom. The same as the last but darker at the bottom than the top. The same as the last but darker at the bottom than the top. Days heap upon us. Where is Violette. Walking without flinching. Doubt crumbles open. It is not a value but a disappearance. We come upon the city in our body. The same as the last. The same as the last. The same as the last. The tint once over in the plain part, and twice in the clouds. Days heap upon us. Where is Emily. Out in all weather. Dignity crumbles open. There is not even a utopia. We would have to mention all the possible causes of her death. The tint once over the openings and twice in the clouds. Days heap upon us. Where is Olympe. Going without rest. The polis crumbles open. This is no different than slow war. The tint twice in the openings and once in the clouds. Days heap upon us. Where is Michelle. Homesick for anger. Midnight crumbles open. The tint twice in the openings. The tint twice over. Days heap upon us. Where is Bernadine. At description. The tint twice over. Days heap upon us. Where is Kathleen. The tint twice. The clouds darker than the plain part and darker at the top than the bottom. The clouds lighter than the plain part and darker at the top than the bottom. The lights of the clouds lighter. The others smaller. The same as the last. The same as the last. The tint twice in the openings and once in the clouds. Days heap upon us. The tint twice over. Days heap upon us. With others smaller. With others smaller.

My purpose here is to advance into
the sense of the weather, the lesson of
the weather. Forever I'm the age 37
to calm my mind. I'm writing sentences here
of an unborrowed kind. The sky is
mauve lucite. The light lies intact and
folded. You can anticipate the wind.
A slight cloud drifts contrary to the
planet. Everything I'm writing about
begins as the robin as the song
sparrow begins is description
animals are description sparkling
scrapping in loose shrieks teenagers also
utopia is memory the broken
bits running motors leaves remarkably
simple and heart shaped and practical
as leaves the gentlest flavour of them is

description and islands of written
stuff love operas and suicides vast
itineraries of error, memory
grey silk sky with pigeons circling
description because memory can't
love as the orange lights of description
beneath the birds which appear to be strings
of memory in speaking of this small
thing, repeatedly to speak of some small
proximity and in what ways the tough
days pass into languor smoke trees brightgrey
clouds moving in Heaven, streets with
clouds or dripping mist, the mist touching the
golden age of untranslatability, no
distinction: just the fear of isolation
from objects and from the clouds, breathing
arguments I wish to touch as
if the touch were emblem of the scene of novelty.
'Tis not my purpose to retrace the under-
thirst, then the severance. I'll finger
sincerity, by exemplum relate
a portrait of my luck.

wednesday

A beautiful morning; we go down to the arena. A cold wintry day; we open some purse. A day is lapsing; some of us light a cigarette. A deep mist on the surface; the land pulls out. A dull mist comes rolling from the west; this is our imaginary adulthood. A glaze has lifted; it is a delusional space. A great dew; we spread ourselves sheet-like. A keen wind; we're paper blown against the fence. A little checkered at 4 PM; we dribble estrangement's sex. A long, soaking rain; we lift the description. A ripple ruffles the disk of a star; contact thinks. A sharp frost and a nightfall of snow; our mind is a skin. A slight cloud drifts contrary to the planet; the day might be used formally to contain a record of idleness. A slight storm of snow; our prosody flickers. A solid bluish shadow consumes the day; we think about synthetics in the night. A soul-thrilling power hovers; we drink it back lustily. It is the exchange of our surplus. A very great tide; lurid conditions enter as fact. A very wet day for it; we loathe and repeat and suckle our sentimentality. April has never lost its leaves; our heart is both random and arbitrary. At sunset red and hazy; we seduce the permanence. At times moderate becoming good; we'll be voluptuously poor. Begone! facilitates our appearance. We go inside rapture. It is our emotional house: A grass green fibre of wool decking cassiopeia. The fourth part of utopia suppressed by the existent horizon. In the real dog hours, conspicuous splendour. The dog who all the signs name Senator. Water, wherever water comes from. Declension of the sky, the caduceus or staff. Capability of nomenclature. A crinoline covered our face. Lyres, serpents, and other luxury equipment. Conspicuous lineage of Greece. Latrines. The quorum as alibi. The sun so situated. Brilliant; equilibrium speaks mysteriously through our larynx. Checkered blue; appetite will be more likely. Cheerful, tender, civil, lilac colours; we anticipate the never-the-less. Clear blue but yellowish in the northeast; we sit and explore. Clouded towards the south; we will not be made to mean by a space. We'll do newness. Crickets accumulate; our expression of atmosphere has carnal intentions. We also do decay. Dusk invades us; the description itself must offer shelter. No gesture shuts us. Each leaf's a runnel; the struggle is not teleological. We break the jar, smack it down. Soul spills all over — cyprine. Every rill is a channel; our shelters are random. Every surface is ambitious; we excavate a non-existent era of the human. Everything is being lifted into place. Everything is illuminated; we prove inexhaustibility. Far into the night an infinite sweetness; beyond can be our model. Forget the saltiness; we tear the calendar of bitterness and sorrow. Here a streak of white, there a streak of dark; we pour the word-built world. In April as the sun enters Aries, the clouds are gold and silver dishes; we make idleness as real as possible. Isn't the hawk quite beautiful hanging quite still in the blue air? We dig deep into our conscience. It all reflects the sky; we disintegrate our facade. It anticipates the dry scent of autumn; we anticipate the same. Our emotions are slow enough to be accurate. It emits a tremulousness; we have nothing concrete. It falls in broad flakes upon the surface; we take account of all that occurs. It goes all soft and warm along the way; we are almost cozy. Is it nice having our ticket handled? Like feminine and serious sensations of being gulped. It has soaked through; we have sheer plastic virtuosity. We flood upwards into the referent. It is a protestant warmth; we reverse it. It is an illusion; we aren't afraid. It is clothed in such a mild, quiet light; we intrude on the phenomenology. It is eight o'clock; casual men shut the architecture. It is intrinsically bright; it is our middle class. Don't notice if we open the life; it is literally the wreck of jewels. It is moody, vigorous and dry; we hear the transparency. A seeing can no longer list. It is no longer the end of a season, but the beginning; the buildings make holes in the sky. What must be believed? We go backwards and forwards and there is no place. No shape is for later. It is obscurely flawed, but it really isn't. It is still daylight outside; kick out the lid. It is sun smoke; we put on grease. Our sex is a toy weather. It is the clear, magnificent, misunderstood morning; we pick up the connections. Toy weathers mean less than we assume. It is the regular dripping of twigs; we deal with technical problems. It is too strange for sorrow; we tried to make the past. It leaves behind fragments; we repeat the embarrassment. It screams sensation; we must be vast and blank. It seems moister; the webbing folds. It strives to pierce the fog which shuts the view; we flow through the loops. We duck into the tint. It translates

Lucretius with a high rate of material loss. It turns decorative; we waste everything. It used our organs; shame was passed along. It was inevitable; we are self-regulating. It washes our beach; we resist agency. We are not free to repudiate. It will go on diffusing itself without limit; our nourishments are never habitual. It will never rain; we feel bad about certainty. It's a fine flowing haze; we don't know light. It's a tear-jerker; we practise in attics. It's almost horizontal; we seem to go into words. It's an outcropping of cumulus; we are a sum of inescapable conditions. It's been a long season; we moot the responsibility. It's brisk; we suggest a new style. It's cold in the shade; we rethink expediency. It's dark as us women; we keep up with accident. The hill slopes up. Our pearls broke. We are watching ourselves being torn. It's gorgeous; we accept the dispersal. It's just beginning; we establish an obsolescence. It's petal-caked; flow implicates us. It's so still; ease of movement is possible. It's very hot and fine; where does this success come from? It's wild; culture will fit now. It's chilly; we try to shape culminations. It's clear and windy and wakening; we achieve an inconsistency. It's starting to melt; we wander, play and sleep. Which is the surface? It's sulking behind blinds; our ideas are luxury equipment. What is beyond? Leaves shoot up; we should not remember it. Light bounces from the clouds; we play at the shelter. What's memory? Fat. Deluxe. Cheap. Listen to the pulsating leaves; everything we make is thick, fat, deluxe, cheap. Look at the moon; we reassess the lifespan of use. Look! March fans it; the conversation is flaring. We're making sounds of sincerity. Marvelous. No sun shining; we feel there must be a world. We avoid the duty of being. One hundred invented clouds multiply sincerity. You can hear radios licking nothing but the entire present, in dawdling chiaroscuro of cause and effect. You're really this classical man hearing a poem, this long voice reeling through chic traditions of green. But you flaunt privacies that split their sheaths. Like rank vegetation running you play walking like a panther when you need stimulation. It's not irony when you moisten our pen. You've always wanted poetry, our slimy harness and soft restraint. Now look; we embed ourselves in immateriality. Of course it rained! We chuck gravitas. Pinkish-green, and grey with yellow tints; look at the thin metaphor. Pockets of fog; compositions do desire. Pulsing lights; our attention is glass. Rain pelts the glass; we seek to produce delight. Skin hinges the light; this is a conceptual war. Smoke ribbons up from the city; we are splendidly desolate. Snow fills the footprints; we abruptly coincide with neurosis. Some tufts are caught in the previously bare limbs; we develop the desire. Something terrific is going to happen; we stick like belief. Space is quite subdued; but not as a result of complacency. It is the great middlediction of concupiscence. Speakable; utility. Spectacular; desolation. Spring seems begun; we like bad palliatives. Storms do occur; manifestoes are the opposite. That's right; disgust is fatal. Enough of the least. Death is a content. The air seems flushed with tenderness; prognostics give us logic. The atmosphere recedes; we simulate failures. The bay's pretty choppy; we allow ourselves to be drawn in. The blue cleansed or swabbed; we are not mimetic. We rhyme. The coldness is purifying; we create an immanent disaster. We shorten the dark. The dark drinks the light; we omitted the beginning. The day is longer now; we're fueled by the thoughtless. The dry light has never shone on it; we excerpt effort. The earth goes gyrating ahead; we frighten the strengths. The fading woods seem mourning in the autumn wind; we don't regret error. It is our emotional house. The fog is settling in; we're sardonic. The fresher breeze rustles the oak; our treachery is beautiful. Pop groups say love phonemes. We suddenly transform to the person. The hills fling down shadow; we fling down shadow. The horizon is awkward; we fling down shadow. The horizon melts away; this was the dictation. The ice cracks with a din; very frustrating. The leaves are beginning; it unifies nothing. The light lies intact and folded; we open and shout. The light seems whimsical; it's techno-intellectual work. The light's so romantic; we permit the survival of syntax. The little aconite peeps its yellow flowers; we manipulate texture. The moon is faintly gleaming; we expose our insufficiency. Total insignificance of lyric. That's what we adore. The mountains have vanished; our mind becomes sharp. The mountains unfurl long shadow; ornament is no crime. The nightreading girls are thinking by their lamps; we make use of their work. We cannot contain our pleasure. The rain has loosened; we engage our imagination. The sentence opens inexpensively; we imagine its silence. The shrubs and fences begin to darken; we are deformed by everything. Therefore we're mystic. The sky is closing in; we mediate an affect. The sky is curved downward; we desituate memory. The sky is dominant; we lop off the image. We come upon our thought. The sky is lusty; so are we. We prove inexhaustibility. The sky is mauve lucite; we reduce it to logic. The sky is packed; it is ours. The sky is thickening; we have been invented. We are the desuetude of function. The sky's tolerably liberal; despite and because of the rhetoric. The snowdrops are starting; we risk causing suffering. The snow going off; by way of the idea. The songsparrow heard; our artifice collides. The sound settles like jargon; we do not agree. The storm is a mass of sound; we must go to the suburbs. The sun is just appearing; we cannot sit waiting. The sun sucks up the steam; it is explicitly our preference. The system shines with uninterrupted light; we generate limpid fact. The systems revolve at an even pace; fear is not harmful. The time is always still eventide; our language moves across. The trees are stripped; foreground fiercely smashing the mouth. The trees look like airy creatures; we'll say anything like speech. The wind has lulled; we're this long voice under fluid. The wind has stripped some nearly bare; we demonstrate abstinence. The wind hasn't shifted; we have shifted. The word *double* is written on our forehead. The wind opens the trees; art is too slow. The wind shifts from northeast and east to northwest and south; we cull the obedience. The wind sounds like paper; our sex is no problem. The elms are as green and as fresh as the oaks; we taste of aerial fluids and drugs. There are curious crystallizations; we are the dream of conflict. There goes the sun; we influence contingency. There is something in the refined and elastic air; we step into the quorum. They are quietly dissolved in the haze; we quietly erect this subject. Thin, fleshy roots of light; we thicken to slang. This greyness is constant; we withdraw unexceptionally. This is a cloudburst; no-one's turn is dwelling. This somber drizzle is familiar; it's unbuilding pixels. This transparency is necessary; there is no transgression possible. Those stupendous masses of cloud! We furrow and sleek and fondle our sentimentality. Thunder in the north; we enjoy our behaviours. Thunder, far to the south; habitual. Today has everything; we are sick with sincerity. Transparent tissues hover; authority flows into us. Try to remember the heavy August heat; we cannot disengage our calculations. Under that rod of sky is our breath; we don't understand love. Describe it again. Up goes the smoke quietly as the dew exhales; it calls itself sadness. Pattern undercuts the slamming heat; we speak into the dark and make corrections: Shadow for Hour. Tantrum for Lyre. Lure for Light. Rapture for Kaput. For for Five. Qualm for Finger. Bridge for Door. Neap for Note. Curious for Lucid. Door for Bridge. Feather for Epsom. Minus for Nimble. Parity for Rapture. Plumb for Addle. Rustic for Cunt. Note for Iota. Item for Opus. Rustle for Campus. Augustine for Aconite. Similar for Ribald. Firm for Forsythia. Resplendent for Respond. Cause for Quote. Oblique for Oblique. Verb for Flex. Superb obedience really exists. When accuracy comes it is not annihilated; we're economical with our sensation. Who has not admired the twelve hours? We offer prognostics. Red sky at night, a warm arm across the pillow, within winter, but at its end; you can anticipate the wind.

Noon was fabulous — the huge clouds
edged the black clouds and may be compared
to *riposo*, non-natural and mystical. Louche
atmosphere branched into the streets
where dissolute I browsed
among trinkets. I eat a date. It is still
only noon. Often I reach to transitory themes,
like "what is there that I can love?" and find
these themes sweet for their own sake, the outcome
not so fascinating. What foliage
is betterment. Dissolute it browses
the mists. I am always wrong
to anticipate the intelligible. What
is your status — pretty
pretty crouching in noon
achieve your record, hurry
down to the deep rolling
surface, the deep rolling face
the faked night of the nightingale; late
song is not me (throwing myself on the
van gently beside battering confessing

is real: washed 2 shirts 1 tablecloth
2 underpants a bra) nobody
was moving I was loving being beautiful
to anybody in the life of the
money the era was circulating wow
it is you — bring lust into the library
or it is hell. Kiss all of it and leave
with no sympathy for habit. Who's
the King? Not I. Who's the mother
but the escape of artifice into sunlight
who morphs into anything, who funds
the disappearance of faces and nouns
who played they ruled the cloudy realm
who's fucking Helen, who said Swinburne
was womankind. Possibles
are not the nightingale. Beatrice
Provence is cold! I repeat. What foliage
is betterment. Dissolute it browses
a dribbling. o gild the age
then the squalid severance.

thursday

All around is the mould of distance. Come we now prefer-
ring. Nothing else is happening. Come we now walking.
Now also be here. Now bending, come we crawling. Now
crisp, come we falling. Now sparkle, eating. Now swagger,
drinking. Now transmit, smelling. Now yellow, sucking.
When a mass, come we avoiding. When by the margin,
come we now ignoring. When clouds go, come we now
tripping. When conditions of freedom come. When cor-
morants play. When corn comes. When dogs lick. When
newness and shame, come we now throwing. When glit-
tering, we're slapping. When gulls are blown jets. When he
is offered we are preferring. When here and there, sitting.
When worthy, walking. When hung, falling. When in
calm, eating. When in Spring, we want to speak in belts of
light. When it comes to regulating, drinking. When
monogamous, besieged. When no perception, doing
warning. When none would, a pip of wet, stillness, a

runnel. When observed from a perspective, we want to be besieged. When occupying, formal, fair of face. When on the southern banks, the entire present rolling, we build our machine of faces. When presented with it, moisten our pen, necessity. When pushed to the wall, art is too slow. When returned, the extraordinary foreignness of the concept, stimulation, inflecting the apparatus. When reverberations, a sleeve. When rounding westerly, play walking like a panther, full of grace. When sex in all its aspects, multiply sincerity. When nerves huddle, an account of totality, need stimulation. When sleep begins, radios licking fun. When summer, like rank vegetation running. When the activity's sufficient, we are capable of designing, form a word like truthful. When the changeful, enter as facts, running secret. When the contradiction, we can't help it, throwing. When the dialogue, it's not irony, surfing. When the dimpled white-hot poplar, enter as facts, gliding. When the heron comes, we sound its little rattle, thinking. When the moon, flaunt privacies, godlets. When the new moon comes in, split their sheaths. When the plan, a purse, optical. When the rain causes bubbles, we want pleasure, chemistries, cogitations, banality, acoustic devices, practical deeds, insuperable, the room in which a death. When the sun, we will never stop. When the surf breaks, soft restraint, a grand condition, laureate, the room. When the surface of things, soft restraint, motility, girls grouped on the lawn. When the trees, licking nothing, greeting fantasy, subsist by these glances. When the white-pinks, we show myself its seam, thanking intelligibility, giving image. When these people are in the world, the sensoria of organs, rubbing and dreaming, shabby with dark, gathering concentration. When they abundant float, her slimy harness, teaching danger, slow affluent. When they break heavily, privacies split, teaching and fading. When they flit in calm, in dawdling chiaro-scuro, lost and won, the image thinking, of woe. When they heard the first note, this long voice reeling, truly vernal, exactitude a girl's. When this factor, in politics, something of strata, largely quickness. When this line of questioning, bossy, rubbing and lunging and dreaming against founding. When threatened, we study everything, no shape is for later, inside the cliché. When upon the mountain slope, translating, wild heaps and shreds, far to go. When vapours rolling, people and days, a brilliance among the media, an inappropriate glittering. When we are convinced, people and days, good rain, lucite days with hail or wind, woods and hills the rind greens, emotions dangling, these little spiritual boughs. When we have crossed a boy, we can't help it, float mid-way above the gifts, discomfort, shoving and giving, proof. When winds are rising, we can't help it, proof. When winds, seeing and generating, silently faces, works hard for its living, proof. For whom are we that form? When women. When women. When world no longer determines, this artificial obscurity. When yoking, moisten glamour. When you're on the sea, nothing else is happening. When, instead of hundreds, all around there is distance. Nothing else is happening. Now crying. All around there is distance, giving and warning. This one's now for Judy.

Sometimes I want a corset like
to harden me or garnish. I
think of this stricture — rain
language, building — as a corset: an
outer ideal mould, I feel
the ideal moulding me the ideal
is now my surface just so very
perfect I know where to buy it and I
take it off. I take it off. If all things fall
and we are just emperors, serious
and accurate and fugitive
in such dormant lines of gorgeousness
the day is a locksmith

dew lies long on the grass
and I a rustic ask: what is
a surface — and respond
only omniscience, the crumpling face
as the domestic emotions elucidate
themselves a sea of mist
exists so strangely side by side
the potent mould of anarchy and scorn.

friday

We rest on the city or water or forms assumed in a fine evening after showers the sky full of the specimens of the peculiar forms. This picture presents the commencement of an evening mist. We rest on the violent events or concatenations of incident or ointments makeup pollen the moving ornament after fact is entered showing rollicking vigorous and wet. Of the sky part a dense body of cloud. We rest on the chthonic pageant or on the satisfying imbroglio in incompletion as in low and creeping mists. The picture is after showers. It means famous glorious and beautiful. In a fine summer's evening. Tacit. After showers. Some needs are only ever complex. We rest on eschatological space or on the long choreographies of greeting and thanking upright upon them as keys. How do we transform ourselves. Laciniation. We are almost transparent. We rest on the rhetorical face. Body of cloud through the night. Now we will be persons. Body of cloud by the fibres collapsing. We rest on erotic heart-love or resist. Now we persons are breaking open. The real is not enough to pleasure us. We rest thrice in the advance of zestful agitation or on the confession of conflict unneedful and hard and as the distant world forbidding within ourselves as rivals. Body of cloud like an inundation. We are sexual peninsulae. Body of cloud from the bottom of buildings. How is it now to be a lady. Tacit. Like the future is relevant. We rest on deep vacation and no sorrow and we speak amazing upward structures plumped. Construct the uninhabitable streets of our life. Body of cloud arrive at their maximum. We rest on the bafflement. Great empty ballrooms of the future. We explore water and air also alabaster pigment and stainless steel. Construct the most radical banality. The hurts felt. New golden face. Body of cloud personified. If we abandon a pronoun an argument is lost. We rest on the fringe of a vigorous architecture fighting and sliding as the orange lights of description therefore we're inflected by the site. Construct the real games and emotions. Blocked soliloquy. Tacit. New face of cold presented. Body of cloud of our minds. We want to speak the beautiful language of our times. Lashed by change. With no memory. Without admonishment. We rest in the shack. Construct texts leaflets and positions taken. Poverty fables. We rest on the tiny-leafed material and resist. Body of cloud of the conventional pieties. Not for whom do we speak but in whom. Umpteenth agony. We rest on the uncertain depth. Speak to us non-responders. Construct so much decoration. Just pour doubt. Body of cloud soft unleashes. Where can a lady embrace something free blithe and social. By our own elasticity. In a perfect calm. From our attraction. On the surface. When the evening returns. Into the atmosphere by night. Attended with a calm. Thrown into the omniscience. By the certain tendency. Next the earth and almost out of reach. We rest tacitly in the flickering of a book or a street as an acute dissatisfaction or in the rapacity of adoration roughened and donating and pouring only omniscience. Body of cloud of work. Where can a lady reside. Next the earth and almost out of reach. Almost always electrified. To surfaces of discontinuity. In light clothes and coloured shoes. By the little flower called the pansy. O little bird extravagant. Among its decayed houses. Against intolerable justice of betterment. Spontaneous body of the plants we tread on. This fig and that fig. Rough boards. Are the streets really secular. We rest on the streets or warnings. Where can a lady reside. Shabby with hungers. About the year 2001 in the grey of dawn. This is perception. Now thickens up. Now parses. Construct the unpredictable equilibriums. Construct false latinities. Construct the touch of risk. Construct the noble. Construct anger.

Construct face. Now soft unleashes. We rest on deep rhetorics. Sometimes what we perceive best is shaded. Becoming ornament. Now swiftening. We speak as if our tremors our postures posed spaces. City of hunger and patience. Floating in calm space. We shall be sober in our imprint. Then go on diminishing. Sober in our imbroglio. The city tacit. At the same time descending. Sober in our orchestra. Grassy — recumbent. With no formal admonishment. Body of cloud laciniated. We speak as if in you alone.

I make a little muscle
to disallow each part; a collar clamped
against the cold, a nail against the rock.
Sometimes, just what I praise, I believe. Words
take a verity to paradise. Some scruple
outside the word works it to leather
a purse for the escape. And tucked therein
each procrastination minified, the indecisions
of rare cash, a very small umbrella
and sullied handkerchief —
but I've misplaced those relics. It is April
my twin and the splendid world achieves
its splendid portrait. Though I'm
but a movement in grammar, I would like some
company, some conversazione
as the blue-green green-gold golden black-gold
silver-green green-white iron-green scarlet
tipped foliage turns black now say
something quite ordinary, morning, say
radiant you're having it having the
place that's volute having wept your
eyes innocuous say you want to be
a popstar, recognized, magnificent

part of danger. What lunch isn't
a trope. What is texture and what is
brutality just socialize your
animal say in the struggle with
spiritual matter play origins of
pleasure an ultra-light mortality the
present insubstantial deep in the
beautiful texture you are modern
subjected to implicit rule say
the sameness of the stories the strands
of attention, obstructions and intensifications
say permanent states of unrest
perhaps the present say what we are
freed into over and over the viscosity
memorize the viscosity memorize
being freed and the birds arranged
in their tree and the pulse beneath
our coats and the pulse beneath this
is the specific exit of love into original beds of blue silk.
Slowly and patiently the tree
crumbles open. The park is present
with us, point-like.
Some of us light a cigarette.

saturday

To language, rain. To rain, building. Think of this stricture so that the vernaculars of causation quicken. To Claude, his contemplation. To objects, passing. To golden change our own blazing device. The day follows the present. Half and then half, delectable and idle, with gleams of fine greenery in the intervals. To the middle of instability, no absolution dad. To the end of surfaces, our mistake. Pop groups say love phonemes. To the middle of the phoneme, people think in belts of light. To the end of pulling, a clangour, a highth, and a name. At the beginning we pinken, require cloth. To the end of moot falsity, hard leather, love. To the beginning of disburdening, the striving face. To the latter end of autumn, the stubborn lung. How are we to unlearn each thing? The next insistence, sullied; thence to the end of insistence, pulling the hard air into the hard lung. Histories, windy, float midway above the dark, and we will insist on wanting. Just for the first fortnight: during the middle an infinite sweetness. To the pigment, a mistake in context. The whole of comparison completely, slowly browsing forward. A fatality with purse. May began with summer showers, and ended with its streets, its underground levels, its frontiers. June, irrealized, chequered with gleams of sunshine. The rights of loneliness don't tear it. The first procrastination, dark and sultry; the latter part merely dirty, with heavy lines. Some tufts are caught in the previously bare limbs, tufts of a genus, a highth and a name. It is a movement as the disburdening of the face. How are we to unlearn each thing? We address you without economy till the last, with sequins and apricots. To the first week of seriousness, just so fucking beautiful: to the end of admonition, it's in you that we shall speak. We're happy and we're picky. So that here is a falling off. To the end of the inflamed limit, we lingered here, encouraged.

So that emotion's a soft anonymity. To the end of the first fortnight in quietness — numerals, minerals and salts. To the end of waking, lust into air dissolving. So that we're above a kind of no-shape. The first fortnight in July only, then go back. To the end of September, we are soloists, float midway above the shabby dark, elaborate. October rainy. November floods upward into its referent. December seeks a runnel. A runnel. A limb. A sky. A disburdening. A highth. A name. A rubbing. A fear. A thing. A fear. A tuft. A face. A runnel. An escape. A number. A wisp. A screen. A knot. A mother. A boat.

porchverse

Read my heart: I enjoy
as I renounce the chic glint
which politics give to style.

From sociology and all
that scorches, I take my leave
now to my theme.

When dog with wren in gorse
I see, the comedy's so human
all lolling in jaw
cheeping like ninnies.

So into hock I go
chanting gently of my memory
presto: heaven earth and
lake, a long pine dock fingering

What's gone.

As the robin as the
songsparrow go as the robin
as the songsparrow go
as the robin as the song

Sparrow go as the robin
is a verse of fashion and
disguise.

That preens the lips which for proximity repeat japonica catalpa
confect slow leisures among leaves as though a gladness
to me, hellebore a winter plant of brownish blossom
hellebore begins, as from a dark divan, this

Description which is Wednesday.

Then refused so lucidly as when
I saw a dog
run a doe
to sea.

Gravity among
the sociological is
not honest.

The porch unclasps each word
of what I say: are these words
perhaps nothing in July?
What makes pronouns, problems

Pedestals? We are lucky
once again, and the socius
of "le texte"
is bullshit.

It is time to paw the
landscape once more as radically
as hard green berries
replace the red and once more

It is too late to be simple.

As the robin as the
songsparrow go as the robin
as the songsparrow go
as the robin as the song

Each leaf a runnel the
roofs now skiffs in green
I've never done anything
but begin.

Thanks to The Canada Council for the Arts, The British Columbia Arts Council, The Judith E. Wilson visiting fellowship at the University of Cambridge, the workers and fellows of Robinson College, Cambridge, and the collective of the Kootenay School of Writing, for generous support. And I am indebted to the stringent and good-humoured readings of various parts and versions of the manuscript by Stacy Doris, Erin Mouré, Lissa Wolsak, Erin O'Brien, Gail Scott, Margot Butler, Rod Smith, Michael Barnholden, and Rolf Maurer. Thanks to Frank Moorhouse for cocktails. To my sister Susan Devine and her superbly lively family. And to Drew Milne and Rachel Potter and Pete Nicholls, extraordinary hosts.

Sections have previously appeared in *Alterra, Gig, Dandelion, W, Raddle Moon, DC Poetry Anthology 2001*, and *Philly Talks*. Thanks to the editors.

The Weather took shape when, wanting to make a site-specific work during my six-month stay at Cambridge, I embarked on an intense yet eccentric research in the rhetorical structure of English meteorological description. I began by listening to the BBC shipping forecasts. Wordsworth's *Prelude* served as a guidebook for the rustic. Mr. Prynne kindly directed me to the work of Reverend Blomefield, an early 19th century Cambridgeshire enthusiast of low and creeping mists. At the Rare Book Room in the UL, Blomefield led to Mr. Wells's *Essay on Dew*, Luke Howard's *Essay on the Modifications of Clouds*, Sprat's *History of the Royal Society*, Aikin's *Essay on the Application of Natural History to Poetry*, and Thomas Forster's *Researches about Atmospheric Phenomena* and *Perennial Calendar*. I devotedly misread Aratus's *Phaenomena* in the 1499 Aldus edition. At the Courtauld Institute I looked at John Constable's cloud sketches, with their written annotations. During a visit from South Wellington, Peter Culley directed me to William Cobbett's *Rural Rides*. Pete Nicholls reminded me to read Hesiod. I found a cheap early edition of Thomson's *The Seasons*. Simon Perril loaned me his chaos theory. Keston Sutherland talked with me about his researches in English georgic. Robert Hampson asked me to talk about my project at Kings College in London. The ensuing discussion was invaluable. Back in East Vancouver, all of these texts, broadcasts, conversations and their rhythms contributed to the composition of this poem. It is weather, and it is for friendship.

Some other poetry titles from New Star Books

Annharte *Exercises in Lip Pointing* ISBN 978-0-921586-92-0
Stephen Collis *Anarchive* ISBN 978-1-55420-018-4
Stephen Collis *Mine* ISBN 978-0-921586-87-6
Peter Culley *Hammertown* ISBN 978-1-55420-000-9
Maxine Gadd *Backup to Babylon* ISBN 978-1-55420-024-5
Andrew Klobucar & Michael Barnholden, eds. *Writing Class:*
The Kootenay School of Writing Anthology ISBN 978-0-921586-68-5
Donato Mancini *Æthel* ISBN 978-1-55420-030-6
Donato Mancini *Ligatures* ISBN 978-1-55420-017-7
Roy Miki *There* ISBN 978-1-55420-026-9
Lisa Robertson *Debbie: An Epic* ISBN 978-0-921586-61-6
Lisa Robertson *XEclogue* ISBN 978-0-921586-72-2
Jordan Scott *Silt* ISBN 978-1-55420-012-2
George Stanley *At Andy's* ISBN 978-0-921586-76-0
George Stanley *Gentle Northern Summer* ISBN 978-0-921586-54-8